1. EMPEROR MAHABALI

Story : **Pradeep**   *Art* : **Sankar**

English Rendering : **C.S. Ramakrishnan**

1 Amaravati is the capital of the king of gods, Indra. It was invaded and conquered by Bali, the emperor of the Asuras. So Indra and the gods had to flee for their lives. Indra approached his Guru, Brihaspati and sought his advice.

Indra, you have attained your position by the grace of Brahma and Vishnu, but you cannot fight and defeat Bali.

The sages of the Bhrigu line have performed yagas and made Bali unconquerable.

Also Bali is devoted to Truth and never departs from justice and fair play. So it would be wise for you and the Devas to remain out of sight for a while.

Sir, I shall follow your advice.

2 Aditi, the mother of the gods, was sad and anxious. Her husband Kasyapa also was very sorry seeing her run-down condition.

My lord, anxiety about the fate of our son Indra is scorching me. What is the way out?

Beloved, attachment to one's son is terrible. But gaining power and losing it depends on His grace.

I shall impart to you the Payovrita mantra given to me by Brahma Deva. You also will get Hari's grace if you practise it. Your wish will be fulfilled.

3 Aditi practised with great devotion the discipline advised by her husband. When the ceremony was over Bhagavan Vishnu appeared before her.

O mother of the gods! I know your want. I shall remove it by taking birth as your son.

4 At that time the fame of Emperor Bali had spread all over the three worlds. He began a horse-sacrifice as advised by his Guru, Sukracharya.

5 As declared by the Lord, Aditi became big with child. A baby-boy was born to her under the star Tiruvonam on the twelfth day (Dvadasi) of the bright fortnight of the month Kanya (September). Even as the parents were gazing, the new-born started growing into the Vamana murti (socalled because he was short in stature). Kasyapa and the other sages performed according to Vedic rules the naming ceremony and thread ceremony for the boy and equipped him with loin cloth, water-jug, staff and other items. Vamana shone brilliantly.

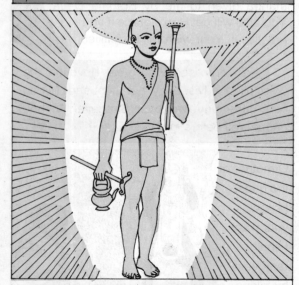

6 With a radiant face Vamana proceeded straight to the place where Bali was performing sacrifice,

The Asuras looked at Vamana with suspicion. But Bali was delighted seeing the lustre on the boy's face. He welcomed Vamana heartily, seated him with great honour, washed his feet and spinkled that water on his own head.

O Venerable Brahmachari! Your frame may be small, but your fame is vast. I consider it my great good fortune that you have come to me. Please tell me what I can do for you.

O emperor of the three worlds! I am a!l praise for the nobility of the grandson of the great devotee Prahlada and son of Virochana who gave up his very life when begged for.

All I want is three steps of land as measured by my feet.

7 O Brahmachari! You are immeasurably great. I am pained that instead of demanding from me a kingdom or even one of the three worlds you are asking only for three steps of land measured by your tiny feet.

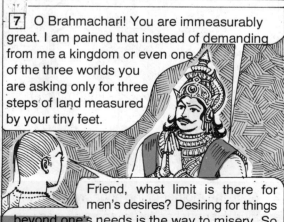

Friend, what limit is there for men's desires? Desiring for things beyond one's needs is the way to misery. So for me the three steps of land is enough.

8 All right. I shall give as you desire. Vindhyavali, please take that water-jug. We shall pledge by pouring water.

9 The Royal Guru, Sukracharya, who was observing all this carefully, now got up.

Stop there. Wait a bit. Do you know who this dwarfish Brahmachari is? Mahavishnu Himself has taken this form and begs of you in order to destroy all of you. So don't give anything by pouring water ritually.

10 Sir, when the Supreme, who can give anybody anything, comes in person and begs, what greater glory can there be than giving Him what He asks for. I have given my word. Please don't prevent me.

Bali, You are disobeying the Guru's advice. You will suffer for that.

11 Bali looked at his wife, ignoring Sukracharya's words. She immediately tilted the water-jug to pour water ceremonially.

But no water flowed.

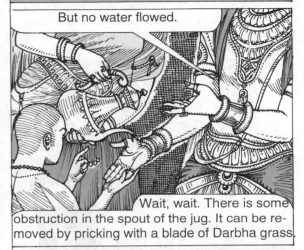

Wait, wait. There is some obstruction in the spout of the jug. It can be removed by pricking with a blade of Darbha grass.

12 Vamana pricked the spout of the jug with a Darbha blade. Lo! There flew out of the spout a bee with one eye blinded.

Ah! One eye has been lost.

13 The moment Bali poured the water Vamana started growing. Raising one foot he placed it on the entire earth.

14 With the second step the whole heaven was under his foot.

O king of the Asuras! With one step I have measured the earth and with the second step heaven too has been measured. Where to place the third step? What do you say?

O Supreme One! Where is the difficulty? I shall never go back on my word. The third step kindly place on my head.

15 Vamana, the Divine Incarnation, placed his foot on Bali's head. As a result Bali and all his followers got pushed down into the nether world.

16 After Bali and his men had been despatched to the nether world, Brahma and Prahlada prayed to the Lord.

O Protector of devotees! Please see that my grandson Bali is not faced with dangers.

My boy, your grandson is not just Bali, but Maha Bali (one of immense might). He has conquered my Maya which few can overcome. His greatness will last as long as this universe lasts. In a future Manvantara (1/14 day of Brahma, about 4,320,000 human years) he will attain the position of an Indra. Till then he will remain in the nether world of Suthala enjoying all good things. I, as Janardana, shall stand guard at the gate of his fort for ever. People will celebrate with joy this day on which he made the great gift.

Lord, you must be gracious enough to grant that I too may reside there with my grandson and have the bliss of your Darsan always.

So be it.

2. JNANESWAR

Story : **Murali Prasad**
Art : **Sankar**
English Rendering : **C.S. Ramakrishnan**

1 Rukmabai lived in a village called Anandi near Pune. One day she was religiously going round a banyan tree. A Saint Ram asrama happened to come that way. He halted, looking at Rukmabai.

She must be going round this banyan tree in the hope of getting a child.

Since a great man has come, let me bow down before him.

2 Rukmabai approached the saint.

May you live long, the mother of many children!

3 Rukmabai smiled on hearing these words of blessing.

Why are you smiling?

You are a great one. Your words can never fail. But I am without the husband who has left me. He went to Kasi to immerse the ashes of his parents in the Ganges. There he took sannyasa from the saint Ramasrama. Years have passed. So what is the chance of my getting children?

4 Ramasrama was taken aback. He cut short his pilgrimage and returned to Kasi. He sent for Vittoba, the husband of Rukmabai.

My son, you never told me that you had a wife. Can a married man take sannyas without the permission of his wife? Go back home at once. If the wife permits be a sannyasi. Otherwise be a householder. Go!

As the Guru commands.

5 Vittoba was in a great fix. He was forced to become a householder, against his wish.

My Lord! Don't be agitated. The banyan tree appeared in my dream and said 'The drama is only to present children who will be assets to the world.'

6 That dream came true. Three boys and one girl were born as aspects of Brahma, Vishnu, Siva and Devi.

The last boy Jnaneswar appears to me to be the manifestation of Sri Narayana Himself.

But it did not so appear to the eyes of the villagers. They laughed, mocking him as the sannyasi's son.

7 Vittoba taught the children sastras so well that people wondered. Yet the villagers made fun of them. The fallen sannyasi has produced stout young ones!

8 I am unable to bear the humiliation of the children. Love, let us go to Kasi.

Ganga will cool our heart-burn.

My father was not interested in family life. He remained a householder only at the command of his Guru. So is it not a great sacrifice? Should he be ridiculed and we be ex-communicated? Can you, the king, permit this?

9 At Kasi with Ramasrama's blessing Vittoba and his wife merged themselves into the Ganga.

My lad, what you say is quite right. But this is a matter for the sastras. Go to the assembly of the learned. Let them give a decision.

11 Jnaneswar, following the king's advice, went to the assembly of the Pandits.

Boy, your argument is correct. But we can accept it only if you produce authority for it from the sastras. Any one may produce the authority from the sastras. We shall agree even if the authority is produced by the buffalo standing in the street.

Vittoba! I give you the fruit of all my austerities. By your sacrifice the Ganga becomes all the more pure.

10 Society ex-communicated all the four children of Vittoba. The younger, Jnaneswar, went to the palace of Ramaraya, the king of Devagiri.

O Pandits! The buffalo also is an aspect of God. It is on the head of the buffalo that Durga Devi keeps her feet soaked in the Vedas.

12 Jnaneswar bowed down before the buffalo and prayed earnestly.

O buffalo, manifestation of God! Kindly show these Pandits the Vedic authority.

Sacrifice is the only way to immortality. This Vittoba has merged in the immortal.

13 Again the buffalo spoke quoting Vedic authority.

By birth all are labourers. The Brahmanas are those that work honestly and discharge their duties.

Ah! How lovely! O, divine! Please forgive our ignorance.

14 Jnaneswar, You have removed the stain that had fallen on your father. You are a realized soul. You are perfect.

Though the eyes that look are two, the vision is single. Jnana and Bhakti are the same. That is Advaita. The Paramatman and Jivatman are not separate.

15 Within his twenty one years Jnaneswar produced three holy books 1. The commentary on the Gita, named as Jnaneswari, 2. Amritanubhav, 3. Haripat.

His greatness spread all over the land. Even today he is hailed as one of the greatest in Maharashtra.

3. MUTHUTHANDAVAR

Story : **Darsana**
Art : **Sankar**
English Rendering : **C.S. Ramakrishnan**

1 Muthuthandavar was born at Sirkazhi.

He is famous because of the many Kirtanas and lyrics he has written on Lord Nataraja of Chidambaram.

In his boyhood he suffered a lot from a chronic illness. So instead of going to school he would go to the temple and worship Lord Siva. He would attend the Bhajan in the house of the devoted dancing master.

Why are you always there in that house? Will song and Bhajan feed you? Look for some means of livelihood.

2 Muthuthandavar paid no heed to such advice. He was charmed by Bhajans.

One day he stayed on in the temple unaware of the passage of time.

Hunger is exhausting. Let me go to a corner and lie down.

3 He went and lay down in the hall where the various vahanas are kept, a spot where people rarely went. In a few minutes he fell asleep. When he reopened his eyes it was dark all around.

The temple doors are locked! How to get out? O Lord, O Mother, You must save me.

4 To praise the Lord he sang some songs from Tevaram. Wonder of wonders! Jingle of anklets was heard. He turned and looked.

What! Is this not the daughter of the chief priest! Even in this darkness she is coming with sacred offerings in a gold cup.

Thandava! What ails you? Why are you sad?

5 Mother, you know about my ailment. Because of hunger I fell asleep.

Don't be afraid. Here is Prasad, eat and be no more hungry. In Chidambaram abides the Lord sporting your name. Have his Darshan and sing about him. Your disease also will be cured.

6 I to sing! I have no education. Mother, don't you know that?

It is knowing it that I am telling you. Go to the Presence of Nataraja. You start singing with the first word you happen to hear there. Everything will end well.

7 The next moment Goddess Uma who had come in the form of the girl vanished in the darkness.

Mother of the Universe! Was it you who gave me Darshan till now! Mother, I shall go to the presence of Nataraja as commanded by You.

8 The next morning two temple guards opened the doors and saw him.

Thandava! What a lustre in your face! How did this gold cup with the sacred offerings reach you?

Everything is the grace of that Divine Mother.

9 He walked all the ten miles to Chidambaram. He went and stood before the presence of Nataraja with great devotion.

Kailasa mountain on the earth!

Which other place than Chidambaram is Kailasa mountain on the earth?

10 All were looking at him. The next line in the song came to him automatically.

Because of the joyous dance of the Lord who gives salvation of the four types- saloka, samipya, sarupya and sayujya.

11 By the time he finished the next two steps of Anupallavi and Charanam of the song Thandavar's ailment disappeared. He stood radiating lustre. One among the audience said:

On the Panchakshara step there are five gold coins. Take them.

O Lord, is it your grace that along with my ailment my poverty too should disappear?

12 For many days Thandavar would go to Chidambaram and have Darshan of Nataraja.

One day it was raining heavily. Flood waters flowed in the nearby river.

O Lord! What test is this? Not seeing you pains me very much.

Sir, I have a boat ready. Please board it, and let us go.

13 As soon as he sat in the boat he had poetic inspiration.

I shall have the Darshan of the Dancing Lord who gives salvation.

I came with the boat only to hear you singing. The song is sweet like honey.

14 Another day he was taking a short-cut and going along a jungle when a cobra bit him.

Shall I get afraid just because a snake has bitten me? My eternal support is the Divine Dancer of Chidambaram temple. I see a special drug in the temple.

15 As he sang, seeing Nataraja with his mind's eye, the poison started getting weaker and weaker. Finally he was able to walk.

The medicine dancing in Chidambaram temple! The drug compassionate to the poor and the devoted!

16 The dance-master asked him one day.

Muthu, You are singing Kirtanas in Tamil. Why don't you give me verses for dancing?

No problem. Let me get the command of the Divine Dancer and I shall sing.

17 He sang as soon as he received the command of Nataraja.

Won't he come in the street! Won't he turn and look at me!

All His grace!

Ah! What a beautiful song?

18 Muthuthandavar lived up to eighty years, singing songs only on Lord Nataraja. On an Ardra day (the star-day of Siva) he stood before the presence of Nataraja and prayed.

My Lord! Show me the grace that you showed to Manickavachakar.

4. NARSI MEHTA WHO SANG VAISHNAVA JANATO

Story : **Srivatsan**
Art : **Sankar**
English Rendering : **C.S. Ramakrishnan**

1 In the town of Junagad, Balaram Mehta was lying on his death-bed. Narsi was his only son. A motherless boy. Balaram was troubled by anxiety about him.

On the death-bed...

O Lord! My end is near. But who will reform and bring up this young Narsi? He is so wicked!

2 This lament of Balaram was heard by his brother, Yamunadas.

Brother, don't worry unnecessarily. Is not your son my son also? Will I leave him an orphan? What if he is a rowdy? I shall see that he grows up a fine lad. Don't worry.

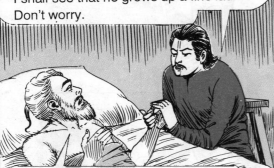

Your wife also is no more. How can your daughter-in-law manage Narsi?

3 Pacified by his brother's words Balaram Mehta passed away. As feared by him, Narsi's wickedness increased.

One day, at play, Narsi tore the shirt of a boy and wounded him. That boy approached Narsi's Sister-in-law along with his companion and complained to her.

Aunt, see how Narsi has wounded me!

Let him come. I shall deal with him.

4 In few moments Narsi returned home quite hungry. Laying the plate,

Sister-in-law, I am hungry. Serve food.

No study! Creating trouble in the village! Rogue! Will you behave henceforward?

5 Beaten by sister-in-law he got furious and ran away from home, from the town itself.

I don't want your food, nor this home or the town. I shall go away somewhere.

6 A forest on the way. Pitch dark. He became afraid. And hunger in the stomach. He looked all around.

Ah! A temple tower there, very dilapidated.

7 It was a neglected Siva temple. Stumbling through the darkness he came to the Sivalinga. In fear he embraced the linga tightly.

God will protect me. Hara, Hara, Siva, Siva. Siva, Siva, Hara, Hara!

8 Chanting Hara, Hara, Siva, Siva, Narsi fell asleep, forgetting fear, hunger and exhaustion.
Even when he regained consciousness He did not give up his tight hold on the linga. He continued chanting Hara, Hara, Siva, Siva.
One dark night, when he opened his eyes who stood before him, but Lord Siva Himself!

My boy, what do you want?

What I want? Don't you know?

9 This is all just forest. This will not suit you. I shall show you a pleasant garden. Come! Look!

10 The dark forest vanished. A bright evergreen grove appeared. There Sri Krishna was playing on his flute, surrounded by Gopis.

Siva took Narsi to Krishna.

Krishna! This boy is my devotee. You bless him that he may spread holiness.

Will Madhava hesitate to bless anyone blessed by Maheswara?

11 Krishna took a leaf from the Tulasi garland round his neck and put it in Narsi's mouth. Hunger disappeared and sacred songs flowed from Narsi's tongue. Narsi began to sing and dance. Krishna placed in his hands a pair of cymbals.

May devotion spread through you.

My boy, Krishna will always help you and bless you.

12 Seated inside the Siva temple Narsi kept singing songs that came in a flood.

Yamunadas who was searching for him everywhere somehow finally reached this place.

Radhe Shyam! Govinda Hari Hari! Radhe Shyam!

Ah! What lovely music!

13   Embracing Narsi,

My boy, whereall I searched for you! Why should you remain here alone and sing? Devotees will gather in great number if you come out and sing. Come, let us go home.

Uncle, is sister-in-law doing well?

14   What of her! Did she not beat and drive away the boy who asked for food? I apologize to you on her behalf.

Uncle, don't get angry against sister-in-law. Is it not through that holy soul that I got this boon?

15   Narsi accompanied his uncle home. He bowed before the sister-in-law who was standing guilty-conscious.

Sister-in-law! You punished me for the wrong I did. That punishment opened the way for me to gain Lord Siva's Darsan and Sri Krishna's grace. What a great honour! I consider you greater than the mother that gave me birth.

My darling! I consider it my good fortune that I was able to bring you up.

16   Narsi Mehta produced a song glorifying Vaishanavism in which there is no distinction between Saiva and Vaishnava cults. Listening to that song men and women melted in devotion.

Vaishnava Janato Tene Kahiye.

The song declares that the true Vaishnava is he who shines as the very image of love, righteousness and truth.
    This is a song beloved of Mahatma Gandhiji.

5. ARUNAGIRINATHAR

Story : **RV**

Art : **Sankar**

English Rendering : **C.S. Ramakrishnan**

1 Arunagiri of Thiruvannamalai was a bright lad, well learned. But when he grew into youth he took to bad ways and fell a victim to disease and poverty.

Even then he did not reform. One day his elder sister Athiamma, pained at his conduct, scolded him. That hurt him so much that he became disgusted with life and ran away from home.

2 Arunagiri climbed up the tower of the Vallalunathar shrine in the Annamalai temple.

O Lord Muruga! Pardon my sins and be compassionate towards me. Accept me and bless me. I am surrendering my life at your feet.

3 He jumped from the tower top. But lo! He did not fall to the ground. Lord Muruga in a radiant form held him in his hands and gently lowered him to the ground.

Arunagiri, my boy! Sing with the name of your grand-mother as the first word of the song

4 Then that radiance disappeared into one of the images. The same instant Arunagiri's ailment also disappeared.

Arunagirinathar began to sing as if the flood-gates had been opened.

Muruga! You are the consort of the one smiling with pearl-like teeth, and the seed of mukti for those who chant 'Sakthi Saravana'.

5 Arunagirinathar took sannyas. Only a loincloth and vibhuti adorned him.

He kept singing the glories of Muruga, melting the hearts of the listeners.

Sister Athiamma came running to him.

Brother, why this dress of yours? If my words have hurt you please forgive me.

No, Sister. You are my family deity. You too have a share in the treasure of Lord Muruga's grace.

6 Arunagirinathar's fame spread far and wide. Sambandandan was the court pandit of king Devaraya. He became jealous of Arunagirinathar's fame. He was a worshipper of Devi and well-versed in Mantras.

O king, who is this Arunagiri? He has had Lord Muruga's darshan indeed! And gained His grace! Can he not give you also Lord Muruga's darshan?

Is that so? Who is there? Bring that Arunagiri here from wherever he is.

As you command.

7 O king, I shall get you the Darshan of Devi. Let that Arunagiri make you see Lord Muruga also. Whoever fails in this test should be exiled from the land.

That is fair. Fix a day for the assembly.

8 On the fixed day the court assembled in a hall near the Annamalai temple.

Let us first have the Darshan of Devi. Then we shall see Lord Muruga.

Here, I shall praise Devi.

9 The assembly waited for long but could not have Devi's darshan.

O king, you can see Devi if you yourself meditate on Her. I shall tell you the method.

Pooh! Is this all! Ha! Ha!

10 Arunagiri! Sambandandan's Japa did not succeed. Now it is your turn. Can you get me the darshan of Lord Skanda?

Everything will happen according to the Lord's will.
Sings Muruga's praise and begs 'May the king's heart be thrilled by the sight of you riding the peacock.

11 No sooner had he finished singing than Lord Muruga appeared on a pillar riding the peacock. The king and those assembled there had a glorious darshan.

O Lord who rules over me! I shall raise a temple for you at this very spot.

12 The Lord vanished the next moment. The king told Sambandandan.

O jealous pandit! You must get out of my kingdom before the sun sets.

Don't, Your majesty! Please forgive him. His jealousy will vanish.

13 Arunagirinathar went on pilgrimage to all the places associated with Lord Muruga and returned after a time.

Meanwhile Sambandandan regained the favour of the king. He got the king to put Arunagirinathar to another test.

O saint! You must get me the Parijata flower from heaven.
Is there anything impossible for you!

As the Lord wills!

14 Arunagirinathar knew the Yogic feat of migrating from one body to another. He left his body at the top of the temple tower and taking the form of a parrot flew to heaven.

15 Sambandandan learnt about this. He went to the king.

Arunagiri realized that he would not be able to bring the heavenly flowers. So he has committed suicide. His body lies on the top of the tower. It is but proper that such rogue sannyasins are burnt up.

All right. Consign Arunagiri's body to the fire.

16 The parrot reached heaven and received the Parijata flower fondly gifted by the gods. It placed the flower before the king.

O Arunagiri, not knowing that you had gone away in the form of a parrot, I believed in Sambandandan's words.
I shall kill that rogue at once.

O king! Don't get upset. I shall remain as a parrot with other parrots for a time and then go to Kandagiri. Lord Skanda will receive me in His hands.

The Lord will deal with those who intrigue.

6. GITA GOVINDAM

Story : **RV**   *Art* : **Sankar**

English Rendering : **C.S. Ramakrishnan**

1 Narayana Sastri woke up from a dream. He roused his wife Kamaladevi.

Lord Jagannath of Puri appeared in my dream and announced that he was blessing us with a son.

Likewise the Lord appeared in my dream also and said that a son will be born of me to write the Bhagavata.

2 Their dream came true.

The elders blessed them that Sri Veda Vyasa himself had been born as their son.

The child was cradled and the naming ceremony was performed.

Let us call him Jayadeva.

3 Even as a child Jayadeva used to sit with his parents and do Bhajan singing the glory of Lord Jagannath.

When he grew up he would go to the Jagannath temple daily and sing devotional songs with great ecstasy.

Padmavathi, the daughter of an elder, Devasarma, used to listen to this with great joy. Narayana Sastri thought that this girl was a fit partner for Jayadeva and united them in marriage.

4 Many would gather in Jayadeva's house and sing the name of the Lord.

Jayadeva began to compose a beautiful hymn called Gita Govindam.

5 Jayadeva happened to write in one of the Ashtapadis (octets).

"Radha! My mind is burning thinking of you. Please cool me by placing on my head your rose-like feet."

What a perverse idea! A girl to place her feet on the head of the all-powerful Lord! What a sin? These lines should go.

6 Jayadeva went for his bath, with a cup of oil.

Padmavathi was tidying the puja room.

Jayadeva came back with oil-smeared head.

Padmavathi! Bring that palm-leaf bundle. I shall complete that octet.

7 Jayadeva finished his bath and returned to the puja room. He saw written on the palm leaf he had scored off:

'My dear, on my head...'

Padmavathi! Did you write anything on the palm-leaf?

No! You came with oil-smeared head, called for the palm leaf, wrote something on it and went back to your bath.

See, there is oil-stain on the leaf.

8 Jayadeva understood that Sri Krishna Himself had come in his form, written like this and gone away.

Padmavathi! You are extremely fortunate. Sri Krishna Himself has spoken to you. I did not have that luck. How blessed you are!

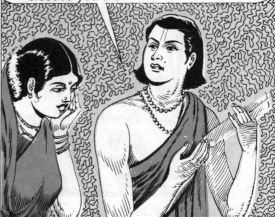

9 A rich man in a neighbouring village invited Jayadeva and gave him prizes. On his way back dacoits waylaid his palanquin. They wounded his arms and legs, pushed him into a deserted well and went away with all the treasure.

10 Fortunately the soldiers of a neighbouring king happened to pass by. They rescued Jayadeva and left him under royal protection. When Padmavathi came and saw her husband she fell down unconscious. Slowly she regained her spirits. Jayadeva consoled her.

Padmavathi! Don't be upset. God has put me in this condition only for me to finish composing the Bhagavatam. I shall start writing it immediately.

11 By Lord Jagannatha's grace Jaya-deva regained his health fully. He finished writing the Bhagavatam.

The work was inaugurated in the temple in the presence of the king and devotees. The Lord Jagannath Himself appeared before them, blessed Jayadeva and vanished.

12 But Jayadeva felt one want. He was sorry that it had not been possible to inaugurate Gita Govindam even as Bhagavatam had been inaugurated.

One night Lord Siva appeared in his dream.

Jayadeva, inaugurate your Gita Govindam without any hesitation, I myself shall help you.

13 The date of inauguration was fixed. Poets and scholars had assembled. The great scholar Kudara Pandita had come from Kasi.

The inauguration began. Some verses had been sung when Kudara Pandita rose up and said...

Jayadeva, you here sing of Radha's feet being placed on the Lord's head. Is it in order?

Ah! What a sin! What a sin!

14 The proceedings came to a halt.

We shall make a test by throwing this work into the Ganga. If Ganga Devi Herself accepts this work we too shall accept it.

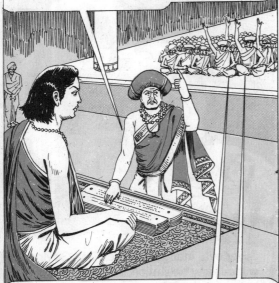

That is correct. We shall do accordingly.

15 A crowd gathered on the bank of Ganga at Kasi. The bundle of palm leaves on which Gita Govindam had been written was thrown into the Ganga. The next moment Ganga Devi rose from the water in the form of a beautiful girl and placed the palm leaf bundle at the feet of Kudara Pandita.

O Ganga Devi! Is it permissible for Radha's feet to be placed on Kesava's head? Do you agree to this?

O Lord! How can you, who are none other than Siva, raise this doubt? Are you not keeping me always on your head?

16 Lo! Kudara Pandita vanished. Instead there stood before them all Siva and Radhakrishna. Jayadeva was thrilled, he adored them.

17 Jayadeva remained in Kasi for the rest of his life singing the Lord's glory. He finally attained Mukti.

Even today his songs reverberate in temples. Legend says that wherever Gita Govindam is sung Sri Krishna makes his presence in company with Sri Radha.

7. POET KALAMEGHAM

Story : **Paruthiyur Santhana Raman**
Art : **Sankar**
English Rendering : **C.S. Ramakrishnan**

1 Varadan served in the temple kitchen of Srirangam.

Mohanangi was a dancing girl in the temple of Jambukeswarar in Thiruvanaikka. The two often met and became friends.

Mohana! Is there no way for us both to live together?

Why not? You leave the service in that temple and come and serve in our temple.

If you agree, tomorrow itself I shall get you appointed in our temple.

2 Varadan, the Vaishnavite, became a Saivite and started serving in the Akhilandesvari - Jambukesvarar temple.

How is it now?

It is great bliss. I was in the brother's house, now I am serving in the sister's house. (Devi is Vishnu's sister)

3 One night the midnight service was over in the temple. Varadan was waiting near the hall to return home in Mohanangi's company.

What is this sound coming from the other end of the hall where a sage is doing Japa to propitiate Devi?

4 Devi had decided to bless the sage. So She came before him in the form of a lovely girl, jingling bangles and anklets, and with mouth full of chewed Tambula (betel leaves). The sage opened his eyes and saw the girl.

Girl, don't disturb my meditation. Go away from here.

All right, I shall go. You meditate. Let us see.

5 Devi saw Varadan standing near the hall.

Varada! Open your mouth. There is no spot in the temple where I can spit out.

6 Varadan opened his mouth without the least hesitation.

The great good fortune that should have gone to him now goes to you.

7 Devi blessed Varadan by spitting the Tambulam into his mouth. The next moment he became an inspired poet: He gained the capacity to compose great poetry.

Mohana, now by Devi's grace. I should sing the 'Tiruvanaikka procession'. Listen.

What glory! What grace!

8 Varadan poured out songs even as the clouds pour down rain. So people began to hail him as Poet Kalamegham.

Dear, if you sing in the court of Thirumalarayar you will get not only fame but also gold and pearls.

Well said. I shall start tomorrow itself.

9 There was a scholar named Athi-madhurakavirayar in King Thirumala rayar's court.

He was very proud and haughty. The other scholars had to carry the many prize items earned by him as he came to the court in a palanquin.

Make way! Make way! The great Athi-madhurkavirayar is coming!

May the great Kavirayar live long! Live long!

Who are you? Why do you stand like a log without praising Kavirayar? What impertinence! Come to the court.

10 The king heard what had happened. He did not offer a seat to Kalamegham, but made him stand.

May the king live long! May your reign be prosperous.

Mother Akhilandesvari! How come this insult to m who has gained you compassion!

11 The moment he thought like this, the king's throme expanded and provided another seat. Kalamegham went and sat on it with dignity.

What magic in this! Who are you?

O king, I am poet Kalamegham who can sing message in five hours and, processions in six in the anthati mode.

12 The king and poet Athimadhura watched in jealousy.

Kalamegham, can you sing Arikantham?

Why Arikantham, I shall sing Yamakantham itself.

13 Arikantham means: A knife would be tied to the poet's neck. He should sing thus. If he made a mistake in his song, the string by which the knife was held would be let loose. The knife would cut the singer's neck.

Yamakantham on the other hand means: A wooden plank would be dangling above a vessel full of boiling oil. The singer should sit on the plank and sing. If a mistake was made while singing, the plank would be let loose. The singer would fall into the boiling oil and perish.

All right. Let us see you sing Yamakantham.

May goddess Saraswati bless me by the grace of mother Akhilandesvari.

14 Kalamegham was able to sing as prescribed and became a hero.

Yet neither the king nor the Kavirayar acknowledged his greatness.

All just magic!

Bliss and grace! What nonsense!

Oh, You say so. May the city of Thirumalarayar, who insulted the Mother, be burned under a rain of sand.

15 When the city was submerged in sand, the king and Kavirayar apologized to him.

Poet Kalamegham, without knowing your greatness we insulted you. Please forgive us and bless us.

16 Kalamegham added glory to Tamil by composing punning verses and many epics. He became very famous. Here is a verse that he sang to correct a girl selling buttermilk.

O water! You are called cloud when in the sky. When you come down to land you are water. And you attain the name of buttermilk when you enter the pot of this girl.

Sir, please forgive me. Henceforward I will not add so much water when I prepare buttermilk from curds.

8. POTHANA, THE GREAT POET

Story : **RV**   *Art* : **Sankar**   *English Rendering* : **C.S. Ramakrishnan**

1 Pothana was born in the village of Ontimitta in Andhra Pradesh. In his tenth year he composed 'Virabhadra Vijayam' and sang it before his mother.

Mother, is it good?

Ah! Is it you who wrote it? I can't believe. How sweet it is! Wait, I shall show it to your father.

2 An elder came to their house one day. The father, Kesana, gave the visitor what his son had written.

Ah! What lovely ideas! What a majestic style! Pothana, my boy, how were you able to write so fine.

Sir, I wrote this by myself. My teacher guided me.

3 Sir, please bless my son.

He is a great soul. How can I bless him? He will sing about Lord Sri Rama and shine as a great poet.

4 The ruler of Rajakonda heard about Pothana's greatness. He sent messengers to fetch Pothana.

Pothana, You may continue your poetic work here itself. Please accept the rewards.

The ruler's wish is my fortune!

5 After a few days...

Your majesty! I have dedicated to you this work called 'Bhogini dandakam'.

Many thanks. You will get all help from my court.

6 As Pothana grew up his wisdom also grew and matured.

So far I have been writing poetry for literary excellence. That is enough. Henceforward I shall sing only God's glory.

7 Ignoring the pleas of his parents Pothana gave up his comfortable career and sat in meditation on the banks of the Godavari.

God will act as my Guru and guide me. Of this I am sure.

8 Once even at the dead of night Pothana did not return home. The parents, searching for him, came to the river bank. Pothana was singing and dancing, completely forgetting himself.

Pothana, my son! What has happened to you? Why are you dancing like this at dead of night, without returning home?

Yes, mother. I am dancing in ecstasy. Sri Rama and Sitadevi came and gave me Darshan. They asked me to sing Srimad Bhagavatam in Telugu.

9 The parents insisted and got Pothana married. The father entrusted his agricultural activities to Pothana.
Pothana would spend the time writing verses on palm leaves.

10 While composing the Bhagavata one day his inspiration came to a halt, and he fell asleep.

Then Sri Rama Himself came and composed what was left blank.

11 When Pothana opened his eyes and saw the new writing on the palm leaf he was taken aback. He wept.

O Lord! You completed my ideas, but I did not have the good fortune to see you.

12 People came to know of this. They took him to the temple and did him great honour. They sent a message also to the king of Warangal.

I am conferring the title 'Poet Laureate' on Pothana.

Take these presents and bring him here.

Let him dedicate his Bhagavatam to me.

13 Pothana refused to go to the court.

This work is dedicated only to Sri Rama. I shall not diminish its greatness by dedicating it to any one else.

Please, take back the presents given by the king.

14 Pothana's wife sent her brother, Srinathakavi, details about what had happened. So he started with his attendants to Pothana's house with a view to give good advice to his brother-in-law. He sent in advance cartloads of food required for all his numerous attendants.

What is this? My carts are returning!

Pothana has sent back all these as unnecessary.

He says Saraswati Devi will provide all that is required for you and your followers.

15 Srinathakavi was an expert in Yoga. He decided to show Pothana his Yogic powers.

My boys, leave the palanquin alone. It will move by itself to where Pothana lives.

16 Pothana and his son were working in the field.

Father, uncle is coming in the palanquin. But no one is bearing it. The palanquin moves by itself.

Is it so? You let go the plough you are driving and free the bullocks also. Come up from the field.

17 Getting down from the palanquin Srinathakavi saw the plough working on the field by itself. He felt ashamed. His pride vanished and he understood the grandeur of Pothana's devotion.

Pothana, I thought of impressing you by my magic powers. You have conquered my pride by the greatness of your devotion.

What of that? Come, let all of us go home.

18 By Saraswati Devi's grace Pothana sumptuously fed all of them after they had bathed in the Godavari.

Pothana, you are not only the Poet Laureate., You are a great soul. It was wrong of me to have tried to persuade you to dedicate your Bhagavatam to the king.

I am leaving now. I shall come with the king for the inauguration ceremony of your Bhagavatam.

Everything will happen as the Lord wills. Good bye.

Pothana, the great poet, sang for the grace of Sri Rama and not for material rewards. So It is that his name shines even to this day.